A DORLING KINDERSLEY BOOK

Senior Editor Jane Yorke
Editor Dawn Sirett
Senior Art Editor Mark Richards
Art Editor Jane Coney
Designer Karen Fielding
Production Marguerite Fenn
Photography by Tim Ridley
Illustrations by Jane Cradock-Watson and Dave Hopkins
Car consultant and model maker Ted Taylor

Eye Openers ®
First published in Great Britain in 1991
by Dorling Kindersley Limited,
9 Henrietta Street, London WC2E 8PS
Reprinted 1992, 1993

A CIP catalogue record for this book is
available from the British Library.

ISBN 0-86318-566-5

Reproduced by Colourscan, Singapore
Printed and bound in Italy by L.E.G.O., Vicenza

·EYE·OPENERS.

Cars

Written by Angela Royston

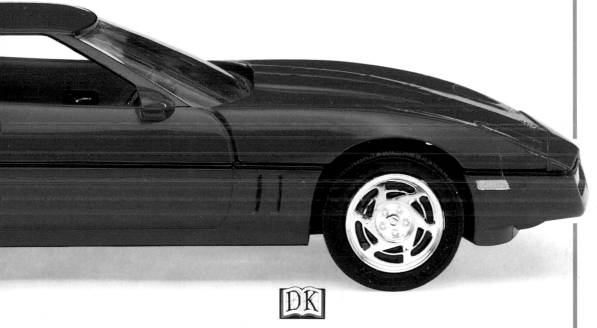

DK

DORLING KINDERSLEY
London • New York • Stuttgart

Hatchback

This small car is a hatchback. The door to the boot lifts up. Inside there is lots of room for bags of shopping. Many families use a car like this to drive short distances around town.

wheel

 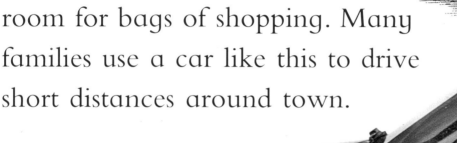

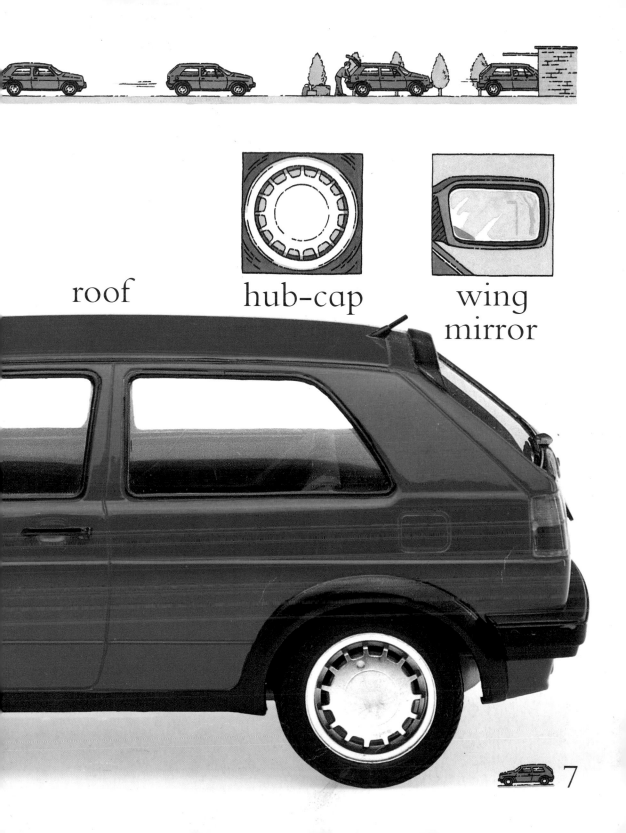

roof

hub-cap

wing
mirror

7

Saloon

This saloon is a big car with four doors. Inside there is plenty of space to sit comfortably. Bags can be carried in the boot at the back. A saloon has a powerful engine that uses a lot of petrol.

bonnet

petrol cap   headrest

boot

Convertible

A convertible is fun
to drive on a warm,
sunny day. The hood
folds down so that
people can drive
along in the open air. If
it starts to rain, the hood can
be put back up.

windscreen
wiper

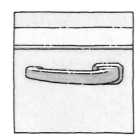

door
handle

exhaust
pipe

hood

11

Sports car

This sports car is long, low, and sleek. It has only two seats, which are close to the floor. Sports cars can go very fast on motorways. They overtake other cars easily.

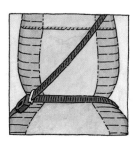

headlamp   seat-belt

boot

wheel

Racing car

Cars like this are made for racing round a special track. They are long and low, and have powerful engines. Racing cars have big, wide tyres. During the race the tyres need to be changed. They wear out from going so fast!

engine

tyre

car body

Vintage car

This car is very old. It was built many years ago when only a few people travelled by car. The owners had a chauffeur to drive them around. Today some people collect vintage cars.

bonnet

radiator
grill

mud-guard

mascot

hood

Jeep

This jeep can drive off the road, across muddy fields or up steep hills. Its big wheels grip the ground and stop the car from sliding. Jeeps are strong and can pull heavy trailers.

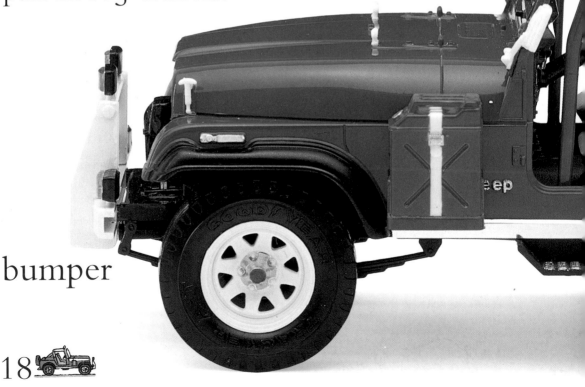

bumper

18

steering
wheel

petrol can

spare
wheel

tow hook

Police car

Police-officers patrol
the streets in this car.
They can be called to
the scene of a crime on
the car's special radio. When they drive fast
they turn on the loud siren and flashing
light. This warns people to
keep out of the way.

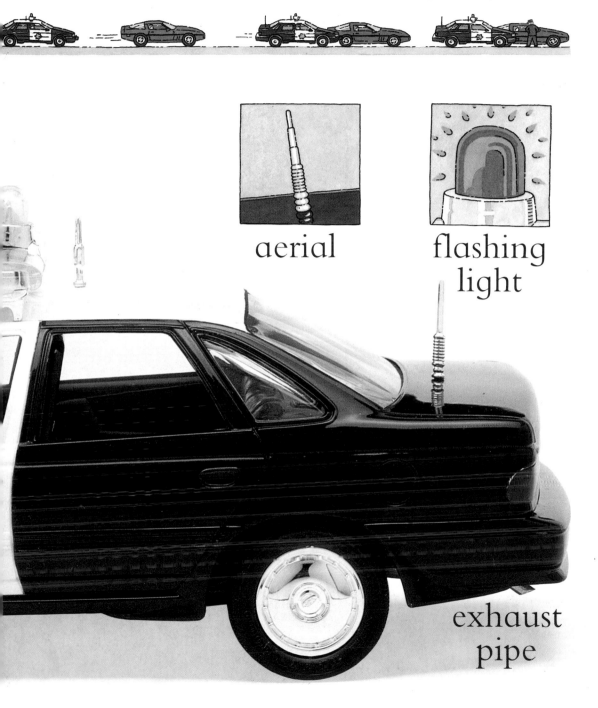

aerial

flashing
light

exhaust
pipe

21

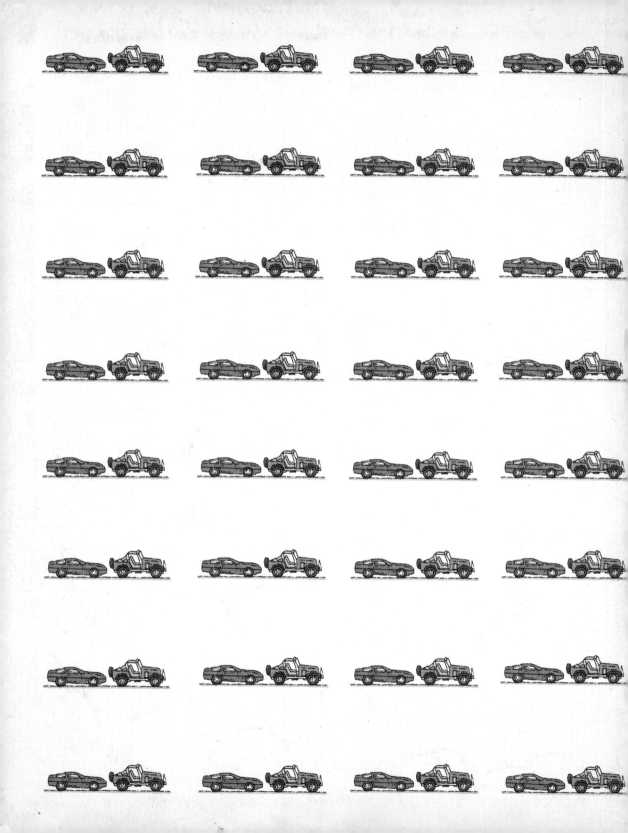